Investigating environmental issues

Fred Martin

Heinemann

www.heinemann.co.uk/library
Visit our website to find out more information about **Heinemann Library** books.

To order:
 Phone 44 (0) 1865 888066
 Send a fax to 44 (0) 1865 314091
 Visit the Heinemann Bookshop at www.heinemann.co.uk/library to browse our catalogue and order online.

First published in Great Britain by Heinemann Library, Halley Court, Jordan Hill, Oxford OX2 8EJ, part of Harcourt Education. Heinemann is a registered trademark of Harcourt Education Ltd.

Editorial: Vicki Yates
Design: Dave Poole and Tokay Interactive Limited (www.tokay.co.uk)
Illustrations: Geoff Ward and International Mapping (www.internationalmapping.com)
Picture Research: Hannah Taylor
Production: Duncan Gilbert

Originated by Repro Multi Warna
Printed in China by WKT Company Limited

10 digit ISBN: 0 431 03254 8   (Hardback)
13 digit ISBN: 978 0 431 03254 2 (Hardback)
10 09 08 07 06
10 9 8 7 6 5 4 3 2 1

10 digit ISBN: 0 431 03261 0   (Paperback)
13 digit ISBN: 978 0 431 03261 0 (Paperback)
10 09 08 07 06
10 9 8 7 6 5 4 3 2 1

British Library Cataloguing in Publication Data
Martin, Fred
Investigating environmental issues
333.7
A full catalogue record for this book is available from the British Library.

Acknowledgements
The publishers would like to thank the following for permission to reproduce photographs:
Alamy Images pp. **4**, **16** (Jeff Morgan), p. **11t** (Fotofacade), p. **13** Photofusion Picture Library, p. **18** (Mark Balgent), p. **20** Robert Slade, pp. **21**, **25** (Justin Kase) p. **27** (Andrew Paterson); Corbis Royalty Free, p. **8**; Corbis p. **28** (Adrian Arbib), p. **9** (Ashley Cooper); Ecoscene p. **26** (Stuart Baines); Edifice p. **10**, p. **11b**; Empics p. **23** (PA/Chris Radburn); Harcourt Education Ltd pp. **6**, **7**, **15**, **17** (Tudor Photography); Rex Features p. **29**, p. **22** (David Hartley); Skyscan p. **24** (Kenbarry); Topfoto p. **19** (Fastfoto Picture Library).

Cover photograph of roads crossing over each other, reproduced with permission of Corbis/Kevin Fleming.

The publishers would like to thank Rebecca Harman, Rachel Bowles, Robyn Hardyman, and Caroline Landon for their assistance in the preparation of this book.

Every effort has been made to contact copyright holders of any material reproduced in this book. Any omissions will be rectified in subsequent printings if notice is given to the publishers.

All the Internet addresses (URLs) given in this book were valid at the time of going to press. However, due to the dynamic nature of the Internet, some addresses may have changed, or sites may have changed or ceased to exist since publication. While the author and Publishers regret any inconvenience this may cause readers, no responsibility for any such changes can be accepted by either the author or the Publishers.

Exploring further

Throughout this book you will find links to the Heinemann Explore CD-ROM and website at www.heinemannexplore.com. Follow the links to find out more about the topic.

Contents

Any words appearing in the text in bold, **like this**, are explained in the glossary.

What is our environment?

Everything that surrounds us is known as our **environment**. It is made up of natural things like air, land, and sea. It is also made up of man-made things like houses, roads, and other buildings. The things that we do affect the environment and how we feel about it.

Your local environment

The area around where you live, go to school, or play is called your local environment. Your school environment is made up of the buildings and any outdoor areas of grass or concrete. There are many different kinds of **land use** on a school site.

The buildings at your school will include classrooms, a library, and a dining area. The condition they are in will affect how you feel about the school environment. There will also be areas of open space, such as a playground, a car park, and perhaps fields for sport. Some areas may have trees or flowers and bushes, play equipment, and benches.

■ *The school environment also includes the noise, the way that people move about, and whether places are crowded or quiet.*

See for yourself

Next time you have a break, take a walk around your school grounds.

- Which places are busy and noisy?
- Which places are less crowded and quieter?

Think about how noise affects people at school. Which noise causes the most problems?

Activity

Study the environment of a small area of land outside your school using the ideas and methods you have learned from studying the school grounds. Find out about the environment of a small play area or park near where you live.

1 Draw sketches or take photos of the play area to show what is there.
2 Measure the area using a tape measure.
3 Using your sketches and measurements, draw a plan of the play area.
4 Make notes about the condition of the play equipment. Think about how safe the ground would be for someone who fell on it.
5 Think about how the play area could be improved. It may need a new coat of paint or some new grass to fill in a muddy patch.

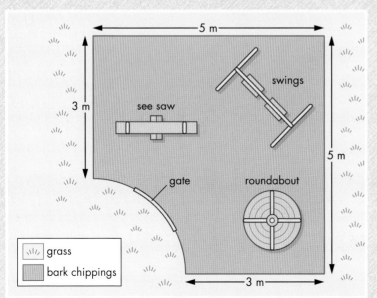

■ On your plan draw symbols for the different pieces of equipment. It is important that you use a **key** to explain what your symbols mean, so that other people can understand your plan.

Loads of rubbish

Waste is anything we throw away. Almost everything we do produces waste that we need to get rid of. This is a big problem for our planet. We have to find places to put all the waste we throw away, and we are running out of space. Some of it may go to a **landfill site** or to an **incinerator** to be burned.

■ *Think about the different types of waste that get put into the **litter** bin in your class. They probably include paper, food, and plastic. Can you think of any others?*

Reduce, reuse, and recycle

We need to find ways to throw less away. There are three ways we can do this. These are known as the three Rs. The first is for reduce, which means buying less of the things that we are likely to throw away. The second is for reuse, which means using old things again, instead of throwing them away. The third is for **recycle**, which means making new things out of old things. We should try to only throw things away when we cannot reuse or recycle them.

■ *There are many different types of waste and some of them can be recycled. Why do you think recycling is important?*

Activity

1 Keep a recycling diary for a week. Write down everything that you could recycle instead of throwing it away.

2 Find out what happens to the following kinds of waste at your school:
- litter when it is emptied from the bins
- waste food from the kitchens
- broken furniture.

Litter and health

Litter makes your school look untidy, and it also causes another problem. Waste food and wrappers attract mice, rats, and insects, which can carry disease. It is important to dispose of your waste correctly, either in a bin or at a recycling bank.

See for yourself

1 Have a look at the arrangements for waste in your school grounds.
- How many litter bins are there?
- Is there any litter lying around the grounds?

2 Draw a plan of your school grounds and mark where the litter bins are and where the litter is.

3 Is there a pattern to where you find litter?

Pollution

Pollution happens when we add things that are harmfull to the world around us. Some pollution is easy to see. Rubbish dropped on the ground and smoke from a factory are pollution. Some pollution is harder to find. Clear, clean-looking water can be polluted with things you cannot see or taste.

Noise pollution

Noise pollution is a sound that you do not want to listen to. There may be constant noise from traffic, trains, factories, or aircraft. Loud music is also noise pollution.

Installing **double glazing** can stop noise getting into houses, but there is very little people can do about noise when they are outside. There are laws to stop people from making too much noise in their neighbourhood.

Polluted views

Things that look ugly can pollute what we see. In towns and cities there are often places where buildings are empty and in ruins. Land like this is called **derelict land**. Derelict land is often polluted by rubbish such as broken glass, rusty metal, and litter.

Sometimes, even something new can look unsightly. A new building may look interesting to some people, while others think it is an **eyesore**.

■ *Would you like to live near an airport?*

Graffiti is writing and drawing on walls. Some graffiti designs can help to brighten up a run-down area. However, other designs and slogans can look bad and cause offence.

■ *This area of derelict land needs to be cleaned up and used in a better way.*

Bad smells

Some places create a strong smell that can be unpleasant. Smells are caused by tiny particles in the air. It is difficult to stop smells from a chemical factory or a petrol station from spreading through the air we breathe.

Exploring further

Go to the Heinemann Explore website or CD-ROM, click on Digging Deeper > **Environmental** change. Read the Digging deeper article 'Dirty air'. Find out what air pollution is, why acid rain is bad for the environment, and what has been banned in order to help protect the ozone layer.

Conserving old buildings or building new ones?

Old buildings are always being put to new uses. It may be easier to change the use of an old building than to knock it down. Whole areas can be changed when their land and buildings are used in new ways.

Conserving old buildings

Sometimes an old building will be **conserved** rather than knocked down and replaced, because its style fits in well with the buildings around it. The outside is kept, and only the inside is changed. For example, in the countryside old barns and stables are sometimes turned into houses. Buildings with a special history are protected because they add interest to an area. These are called **listed buildings**.

■ *This building was once the headquarters for Michelin tyres, it is now a shop and a restuarant.*

Activity

Find out about a building in your town or city that is listed.

1 What was it used for when it was first built?

2 What is it used for now?

3 How has the building been changed?

Changing docklands

In the past, ships used to sail up river **estuaries** into **ports**. They tied up at **quays** to load and unload their goods. Factories and **warehouses** were built beside the quays to make and store the goods. The whole area was called a **dockland**.

When ships became bigger, they needed deeper water and more space and could not reach so far upriver. Often, the old docks closed down and new docks were built nearer the sea. The buildings were left empty, the quays were abandoned land and the whole dockland became **derelict**.

Over the last thirty years, old docklands have been put to new uses. Some of the buildings have been knocked down and replaced with new houses and offices. Many of the most interesting buildings have been conserved and put to new uses. Old dock areas are now places where people live in luxury apartments and work in smart offices.

The docklands are also places where people now go for fun. Museums, theatres, restaurants and shops, hve been built on the land that used to be derelict. Liverpool, Bristol and London are three cities where old docklands are now busy places again.

■ *Liverpool's Albert docklands, showing the transformation from derelict buildings into smart new offices, museums, galleries, and restaurants.*

Exploring further

On the Heinemann Explore website or CD-ROM go to Resources > A better environment. Watch the video on 'Liverpool's Albert Docks' to see how this area is used today.

Traffic problems

It is good to be able to travel to different places. The growing amount of traffic on the roads, however, causes huge problems. Traffic can make life unpleasant for people in the UK.

Increase in traffic

There are about 24 million cars in the UK – that is about one car for every family. A quarter of all families in the UK now own two cars. Some families even have three cars. There are also about half a million lorries, buses, and other types of vehicle. The numbers keep rising every year.

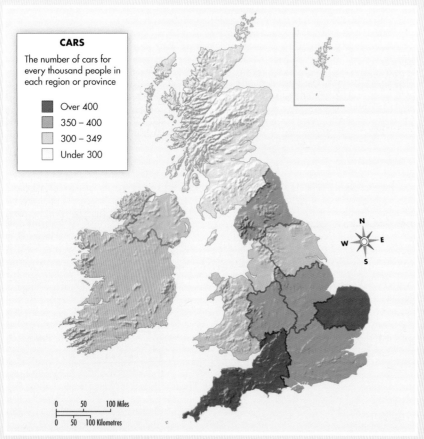

CARS

The number of cars for every thousand people in each region or province

- Over 400
- 350 – 400
- 300 – 349
- Under 300

0   50   100 Miles

0   50   100 Kilometres

■ *This map shows the number of cars on the roads in the UK. Which places would be the worst to travel through?*

The more cars there are, the more crowded the roads become, so the longer it takes to get about. The worst traffic problems are in cities during the **rush hour**. There is not usually enough space in towns and cities to make the roads wider without knocking down people's homes. People often end up sitting in **traffic jams** feeling angry.

Finding a solution

There are lots of things people can do to avoid sitting in a traffic jam. Think about a journey you make regularly by car. Can you think of a different way to travel? If you lived close enough to where you were going you could walk, or maybe you could ride your bike on a special cycle route. There might be a bus or train that you could take, or you could share a lift with a friend. These are all ways of reducing the number of cars on the road. If everyone tried to use alternative transport the number of cars on the roads would be reduced and the traffic problems would be less serious.

■ *Cycling is a good alternative to driving in a car.*

Activity

1 Think about why sharing cars is a good idea.
2 Design a poster to persuade people to share cars. It will need an eye-catching headline to draw people's attention to it.

Traffic problems on the high street

What is the high street like?

The high street in a town or city is likely to be very busy throughout the day. In a small town, there may be only one high street. Larger towns and cities can have many local high streets, each serving the people living in different parts of the area.

High street land use

Most buildings in the high street are shops. In bigger towns and cities the shops are mostly **specialist shops** for goods such as clothes and shoes. In smaller towns, and in shopping centres in the **suburbs** of big cities, there are shops that sell goods that people buy more often, such as food.

High streets also have businesses providing **services**, such as estate agents, banks and restaurants. There may also be public buildings such as a church, town hall or library.

See for yourself

1 Visit the high street in your nearest town or city and have a look around.
2 Note down the types of shops and businesses there.
3 Draw a plan of your high street, like the one below.

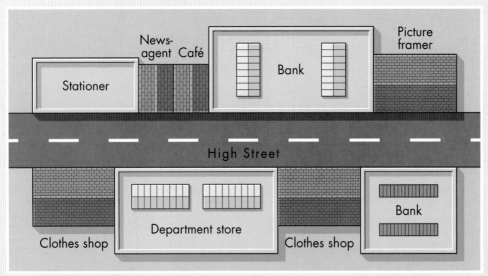

■ *A plan of the shops along a high street.*

A busy place

The high street is one of the busiest places in the town. People come to it from all over the town to buy goods and use the services it provides. Others come to work in the shops, services, and nearby offices. It can get very crowded. Some people travel to the high street by car. This can cause traffic and parking problems.

■ *Kings Heath High Street is in a suburb of Birmingham. There are many supermarkets and smaller shops there. There are also services such as banks, travel agents, and a library. The high street is always busy during the day with buses, cars, and people.*

How big an issue is traffic?

Too much traffic in the high street brings problems. Heavy traffic can make it difficult to cross the road, and delivery vehicles can make it difficult to reach the shops. Problems like this can put shoppers off visiting the high street.

Too many cars

Cars and other vehicles cause **noise** and **air pollution**. These are made worse because the traffic usually has to move slowly down the high street, due to pedestrian crossings, traffic lights, and cars pulling in to and out of parking spaces.

■ *Too many cars travelling along the high street creates* **traffic jams**.

Often, much of the traffic is not even visiting the high street. It is **through traffic**, using the main road on its way to somewhere else.

See for yourself

1 Visit your local high street and look at all the traffic problems.

2 Count the number of vehicles that pass in five minutes. Record this information.

3 Note down how the traffic is controlled. Are there traffic lights, a bus lane, or a roundabout?

4 Are these ways successful? What other ways could be used?

Problems for shoppers

People who go shopping like to be able to park their cars near the shops. This takes up space, either along the side of the road or in car parks.

If there is nowhere to park near the high street, people may decide to go to an out-of-town supermarket where they can park for free. If too many people do this, the high street shops lose their customers and have to close down. If the shops close, the services near them will also have to close.

- *Roadside parking in a high street can be dangerous, because it makes it difficult for drivers to see people who are trying to cross the road.*

Activity

1 Make a list of all the different kinds of people who need to park near the shops.
2 Make another list of the different ways that shoppers are affected by traffic on the high street.

A serious problem

The problems of traffic are difficult to solve. On one hand, people need to be able to get to the shops and other services in the high street. On the other hand, too much traffic can make shopping an unpleasant experience and can cause the shops and other businesses to close down. This is bad both for the shoppers and for the people who own and work in the shops.

17

Should the high street be closed to traffic?

One answer to the problem of traffic in the high street is to close it to vehicles altogether. Before you make a decision like this, you need to think carefully about what the effects would be.

The advantages

In a high street without traffic people can walk more easily and safely between the shops. Cafés can set up tables for people to sit outside and have a break in the sunshine. Stallholders can set up market stalls where the road used to be. This can make the shopping centre a more interesting and colourful place to visit. If it is a more pleasant place to visit, the shops get more business and new shops will open. This gives people a better choice of things to buy.

■ A **pedestrianized** high street is quieter and the air does not smell of traffic fumes.

Activity

Have a class debate on whether traffic should be allowed on the high street in your area.

1 Make a list of as many arguments as you can think of both 'for' and 'against' allowing traffic access to the high street.

2 Compare your answers with those of your classmates.

3 Take a class vote on it.

The disadvantages

Now think about any possible problems if the high street is closed to traffic and people cannot park close to the shops. People may decide to go to an out-of-town **superstore** instead, where parking is free and plentiful. Also, how will the shops receive deliveries of goods?

If the high street is closed to traffic, where will the traffic go? If it goes around the high street, it brings problems to the people living along the new route. Making one street quieter can make several other streets noisier.

- *If lots of people avoid the high street by shopping at out-of-town shopping centres, many high street shops are forced to close, because they make less money.*

How do you solve the problem of traffic on the high street?

It is easy to block off a high street so that cars and other vehicles cannot drive through it. However, it is not so easy to find a new route for the traffic.

Diverting the traffic

The high street is usually in the centre of a town or along a main road that leads to the centre. It is often one of the most built-up parts of the town. This makes it difficult to find a new route for the traffic, as there may not be any land available to build a new road on.

Another option is to divert the traffic on to another road. This road will usually have to be widened and improved to cope with the amount of new traffic using it. The new route must be chosen carefully, because people may live along it.

■ One way to keep the traffic moving through a busy town centre is to create a one-way system. Traffic goes in one direction along one route, and in the other direction along a different route. However, this means finding two routes instead of one, so even more people can be affected.

High street access

Some people will always need to bring their vehicles close to the high street shops. Lorries need to bring stock to the shops, and sometimes to take it away to deliver to customers. How could this problem be solved? Vans and lorries could be made to go to the back of the shops, instead of to the front. Or they could only be allowed to go to the shops in the early morning or evening, when the high street is quiet.

Disabled people also need to park close to the shops, so they do not have to walk or carry their shopping too far.

In some high streets, the only vehicles allowed access are buses. This is to encourage people to leave their cars at home and to use **public transport** instead.

■ *Bollards in this road are raised and lowered so that only buses can pass through.*

Activity

Hold a class debate on the issue of traffic on the high street, and try to arrive at a solution.

1 Think about all the different types of people affected: shopkeepers, delivery drivers, shoppers, pedestrians, workers, etc.

2 Visit your local high street and map the area around it to see if you think your solution will work.

Constructing a bypass

Why does a town need a bypass?

The main roads between cities often pass through small towns and villages. This slows down the traffic, and also affects the people living in the towns and villages. The traffic causes **noise** and **air pollution**.

Building a bypass

One way to take the traffic out of towns and villages is to build a **bypass**. This is a new road that takes the **through traffic** around the outside of the town or village, instead of through it. Although this may seem an easy answer to the problem, it is not that simple. There have been several planned bypasses in the UK where local people have protested to stop the new road being built. They do not want to see the countryside spoiled by new roads.

■ *The busy A34 road no longer goes through the centre of the town of Newbury, in Berkshire. Instead, it flows around the town on a **dual carriageway** bypass. For years, some people protested against the bypass, to try to save the countryside along its route. In the end they lost, and the bypass was built.*

See for yourself

If there is a bypass near you, ask an adult to drive along it. What effect do you think the building of the bypass had on your town or village? Think about both the good and the bad points.

What are the issues involved in building a bypass?

There are many issues to consider before a bypass is built. What is best for the motorists? What would the effects be on the people who live in the town, and on the people who live where the bypass is to be built?

Some people benefit from a bypass, for example the people living along the main road that passes right by their homes. But bypasses also create new problems. They can ruin farmland and take the traffic nearer to other people's houses. Some houses may even have to be knocked down to build the new road.

■ *These people are protesting about a proposed new bypass around Linslade in Bedfordshire.*

Activity

Use reference sources, such as textbooks, the Internet, and old newspapers, to find information about proposed bypass schemes and people's reactions to them.

Where is the bypass located?

A road map or Ordnance Survey map will show you the route of a **bypass** around a village or town. You can also see it by looking at **aerial photographs**.

- *This aerial photograph shows the location of the bypass around the city of Edinburgh in Scotland. Why do you think it was built around the south of the city?*

The best route

The route of a bypass needs to be away from the village or town so that it does not pass through **residential areas**. It also has to avoid going through another village. For drivers, the route should be as short as possible. A longer route will take more time and use more petrol.

Why is the construction of the bypass an issue?

A new road, such as a bypass, affects how people go about their daily lives. A bypass becomes an issue when there is disagreement over whether or where it should be built. People might object to the route of the bypass or the fact that it will destroy the countryside of an area.

Make your views known

People in the UK have a right to make their views known about changes to their area. There are several ways to do this. One way is to contact your local town or county **councillor** or your Member of Parliament (MP). They may be able to influence the decisions that are taken.

Another way is to form a local action group to protest against or to support a new plan. You can also make your views known by telling a newspaper or television company about it. Their job is to report the news. It makes interesting news when people want to protest about an issue.

■ The shape of the land has a major effect on where a new road can be built. A route through a valley is easier and cheaper to build than a route that goes up steep slopes and over hills. The choice of route is also affected by the cost of building bridges, tunnels, **embankments**, and **cuttings**.

Exploring further

On the Heinemann Explore website or CD-ROM select the activity 'Where is the bypass located?' to investigate six cities in the UK where bypasses have been built.

How did the issue of the bypass arise?

The issue of whether to build a **bypass** usually begins with a growing problem of **through traffic** in a town centre or along a village's main road. There are likely to be more traffic accidents, as well as more **noise** and **air pollution** from car and lorry **exhausts**.

- *Drivers who have to pass through small towns and villages are often frustrated by **traffic jams**.*

Activity

Imagine that you live in a small village between two towns. You are spending more and more time every morning in traffic jams, and you are worried about the safety of the people in your village. Write a letter to the local council suggesting that they build a bypass round the village. Give plenty of reasons why the bypass should be built.

Losing business

Not everyone may agree that a bypass is a good thing. People who own businesses in the town centre, such as petrol stations, shops, public houses, and restaurants, can lose their customers when a bypass is built. This is because drivers no longer pass through the town centre.

Losing the countryside

Fields and woodland are lost when a new bypass is built. Sometimes rare plants and wildlife are destroyed.

■ *Farmers can have their farms divided in half by a bypass. This makes it difficult for them to move machinery and animals from one field to another.*

Losing homes

People can lose their homes when a bypass is built. New roads do not usually have sharp bends, and it may be impossible to find a gently curving or straight route through the countryside without passing through an existing house. If a bypass plan is agreed, the people will have to move out of their home.

What groups are involved in the issue and what are their views?

Many different groups of people become involved in the discussions about building a **bypass**. For some, their job depends on it. Others are involved because it will affect their quality of life. The bypass may make life better for some people but worse for others.

Those in favour

Some local people may want the bypass to be built because they are affected by the traffic that goes past their homes. Others may want to get traffic out of the town centre because they think it will make it a more pleasant place for people to shop. Motoring organizations, such as the Automobile Association (AA), want to make it easier for people to drive from place to place. They are likely to be in favour of a bypass.

Those against

Farmers and people living along the route of the bypass are likely to object to it. The new road may mean they will lose their land, perhaps even their homes. They may also be concerned about the way the bypass will affect the **landscape** and its wildlife.

When a new bypass was planned for the town of Winchester in Hampshire, thousands of people protested about the loss of attractive countryside in the area. They wanted to save the wildlife and plants on the chalk hills of Twyford Down. In the end, the new bypass was built.

■ *Some protestors lived in trees to stop builders working on the Winchester bypass. They were called 'eco-warriors'. These kinds of protest are often the best way to get the attention of the newspapers and television.*

Activity

Make a chart to explain which of the following groups of people will be in favour of a bypass and which will be against: a road construction company, town centre shopkeepers, farmers, **environmentalists**. Give reasons for your answers.

How can the issue be resolved?

Nobody wants their local **environment** to be ruined by traffic, but they also do not want the countryside to be ruined by new roads. There are no easy answers to this problem. If more people used **public transport** or alternative means, such as cycling, there would be less **pollution** and no need to build new roads through the countryside.

■ *Even when there is a bus or train service, most people prefer to travel in their own car. Why do you think this is?*

Glossary

aerial photograph picture taken from the air

air pollution bad smells or harmful substances in the air we breathe

bypass road that takes the through traffic around a town or village instead of through it

conserve to save for future use

councillor person who sits on a council to make decisions

cutting passage cut through a hill for a road or railway

derelict land place where buildings are empty and in ruins and the land around them is scattered with rubbish of all kinds

dockland area of industry close to a port

double glazing windows with two layers of glass to keep heat in or noise out

dual carriageway road with at least two lanes in each direction, usually separated by a central reservation

embankment slope of rock or soil that rises from either side of a road

environment natural and man-made things that make up our surroundings

environmentalist someone who tries to protect the environment

estuary place where a river flows into the sea

exhaust fumes produced by vehicles

eyesore something unsightly or ugly

graffiti writing and drawing on walls with spray paint

incinerator machine that burns rubbish

key panel to explain the features on a map or graph

landfill site area where rubbish is stored

landscape scenery and its features

land use what an area of land is used for

listed building building with a special history that is protected and cannot be knocked down

litter rubbish

noise pollution noise that causes a nuisance to people

pedestrianized designed for use only by pedestrians, not cars

pollution noise, litter, smells, or something dangerous in the air or water

port place on the coast or on a large river where ships load and unload their cargo

public transport vehicles, such as buses and trains, that carry large numbers of people

quay place beside a river or the sea where ships load and unload their goods

recycle   to reuse materials, such as glass, paper, and plastic

renovate   to renew something and use it again

residential area   place where people live

rush hour   the times when people are travelling to work or school in the morning and going home in the evening

services   businesses, such as estate agents, banks, travel agents, restaurants and cinemas

specialist shops   shops selling goods, such as jewellery, clothes and shoes

suburb   built-up area on the outside edge of a town or city

superstore   large, out-of-town shop

through traffic   traffic passing through a place

traffic jam   queue of stationary or slow-moving traffic

warehouse   building used for storing goods

waste   rubbish of all kinds that we need to get rid of.

Find out more

Books

You can save the planet, Neil Morris (Heinemann Library, 2005)

Green files: Waste and recycling, Polluted planet, Steve Parker (Heinemann Library 2004)

Discovering geography: Pollution and conservation, Rebecca Hunter (Raintree, 2003)

Websites

www.ollierecycles.com/uk
Learn how you can help the environment by recycling your waste. Play the games, have a go at the puzzles, and look at the facts and figures.

www.wastewatch.org.uk
This site promotes reducing, reusing, and recycling in the UK.

www.highways.gov.uk/roads
Find out from this website where the new roads are going to be built in the UK

Index

Titles in the *Explore Geography* series include:

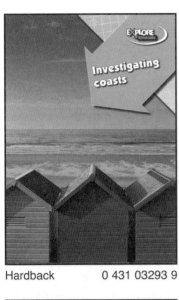

Hardback   0 431 03293 9

Hardback   0 431 03254 8

Hardback   0 431 03257 2

Hardback   0 431 03252 1

Hardback   0 431 03251 3

Hardback   0 431 03253 X

Hardback   0 431 03256 4

Hardback   0 431 03255 6

Find out about other titles from Heinemann Library on our website www.heinemann.co.uk/library